I0467296

Top-Down Technicals

Macro Trading, The Yen 2012

ARUN S. CHOPRA
CFA, CMT

ISBN: 1499615000
ISBN 13: 9781499615005

Library of Congress Control Number: 2014901732
CreateSpace Independent Publishing Platform
North Charleston, South Carolina

Table of
Contents

Introduction

This smaller publication will build on my main work, *Top-Down Technicals, A Historical Guide to Long-Term Chart Setups* and will discuss in detail ways to take existing market information and generate new macro-based trading and investment ideas. I take excerpts from past editions of my monthly investment publication 'The Tape" and combine them with a more detailed look at an entire macro setup creating a total asset class view of what I consider to be a top-down technical cycle. In this publication, I clearly indicate where real-time charts and analysis from 'The Tape' were provided to my readership and where I recreated periods. By recreating events, insight into the main macro event can be increased and utilized in future market set ups. This first 'Market Observation Series' book publication is designed to further highlight my methodologies, my monthly letters' successes, and to expand readers' thinking about how a setup in a particular asset class can affect related markets. In other words, its goal is to aid readers in expanding upon simple long-term trading levels and introduce new concepts that leverage the knowledge of how assets trade relative to one another based on macroeconomic principles.

Chapter 1

THE YEN 2012

The macro setup in this example was a potential top in the yen in late 2012 and the impact on related assets, primarily Japanese equities, that such an event would have. I will discuss how to profit from such a move without a futures account and how to use technical information from new products such as Exchange Traded Funds (ETFs) and leveraged ETFs to increase traders' overall confidence levels. I'll also take a look at the impact of the event on various related markets a year after I first identified the setup.

From a fundamental macroeconomic perspective, by the time this potential market event was technically setting up, it was clear the yen was too pricey from a policy standpoint. The Bank of Japan (BOJ) had already intervened in the currency markets over the previous year, and deflation was clearly the main threat to the Japanese economy. At the global macro level, the strengthening yen was also unwinding the carry trade, thereby depressing other asset prices. Unwinding carry trades generally trigger the sale of risk assets and repayment of borrowed currency, which for the most part had been the yen. The carry trade has been replaced by the dollar over the years as a funding currency, but traditionally speaking, Japanese markets yield the lowest interest and have been used by carry traders for funding global assets. This was important in the overall setup because BOJ intervention at that point was thought to benefit most markets. making action increasingly likely.

Given this set up, the question of 'when' still was critical, as the yen had been rallying since 2007 and was stubbornly locked in the upper ranges. A multi-time frame, multi-asset, top-down technical process is a great way of timing these larger macro events that the market "knows" to be high probability. Market participants can then look at the various ways of capitalizing in multiple markets, sectors, and individual issues based on known economic relationships and detailed technical analysis. By focusing on major global markets, asset classes, and utilizing longer-term time frames, we can better stabilize the probabilities in terms of technical price action.

Section 1: Long-Term Trend, Equity Markets, Publication Excerpts

The top-down process first looks for broad trends as the major macro drivers. This is the longest and most reliable view of trends. I focus on twenty-five-year monthly charts (or beyond) to get a clean look at trends. From there, I zoom into shorter time frames and overlay indicators to get a better idea of timing. In the shorter term, I review weekly charts before moving on to daily charts.

Below are excerpts from my September 24, 2012, publication, three weeks before the top in the yen, and a walk-through of a top-down technical setup. Figure 1.1 shows both the longest-term view I monitor on a monthly basis and the main setup.

September 24, 2012, publication "The Tape"

"The real battle right now is the dollar/yen. Here is the 20 year monthly look at the yen...

THE YEN 2012

"See the large triangle consolidation, the multi year breakout and wedge and now the breakdown."

Figure 1.1

Japanese Yen, 1992–2012, Monthly Chart

After examining the longest-term view and the main setup, I like to zoom in on the price action I am monitoring or on the action that seems most relevant to the setup. Given that this was a multiyear uptrend, with a bearish wedge that seemed to be beginning to break down, this was the area I most wanted to see. Potential BOJ intervention, the fundamental concerns of the banking system, and the general overvalued nature of the yen was the context for what might have been setting up on the longer-term charts. Figure 1.2 focuses on the multiyear uptrend.

September 24, 2012, 'The Tape' continued...

"7 year weekly yen. Zoom in of the uptrend since 07, the trend line has broken and the moving average has turned sideways. What is important here is see the big break of the trend. The BOJ simply could not allow this price to continue to rise..."

Figure 1.2

Japanese Yen, 2006–2012, Weekly Chart

Of note in figure 1.2 ("The Tape" excerpt), especially in terms of taking a top-down view of the market, is that this view of the currency fit my longer-term understanding. That includes longer-term price levels, and longer-term price action. A multi-year weekly chart, with actionable price movement fits within the bigger picture parameters. As noted in chapter 3 of *Top-Down Technicals, A Historical Guide to Long-Term Chart Setups* the fifty-week moving average can be used as a level for actionable price formation to take hold.

This action is the reverse of the bull side and moving averages shown in *Top-Down Technicals, A Historical Guide to Long-Term Chart Setups.* The chart shows the yen breaking through the support indicated by both the fifty-week moving average and multiyear trend line. Here we see a breakdown and a retest of those key levels. Of note is the slope of the moving average, which had clearly turned sideways, increasing confidence that the setup was bearish.

Moving on to the main point of this book, macroeconomic analysis and relationships, the next part of this overall setup is to examine the underlying equity market. This is because of the high level of impact the yen has on the overall performance of equities in Japan. Continued from my September 2012 "Tape" publication:

"Another way to understand this is by looking at the Nikkei. See the big breakout in equities as the currency broke its long-term trend line last year. The market has come all the way back in as the market for Yen has remained strong even with the trend line break on the underlying currency."

Figure 1.3

Tokyo Nikkei Average, 2010–2012, Daily Chart

The next step is to get more data with a much closer look at the weekly price action overlaid with volume indicators on the yen. After the trend and potential setup are identified, the primary concerns are the candle formations and volume patterns. One way to do this is to use an ETF that follows the underlying asset, assuming there is one with decent liquidity. In this case, I took the previous two years on a weekly basis for FXY, the yen ETF.

September 24 "The Tape" continued...

"Last week's trading in the Yen therefore was extremely important. Here is a zoom in of the currency. I have long been looking for a short, here is the 2 year weekly chart. See the

inverted hammer two weeks ago on the ETF. Last week looked to be the reversal, however this week we are heading back up again. This is a curious case, where the monthly, weekly, and even daily charts all agree, but the market will not break. This is unsustainable in my opinion but the trade reminds me of the Short Euro trade, obvious and crowded."

Figure 1.4

FXY, Japanese Yen ETF, 2010–2012, Weekly Chart

The key here is to focus on what is important in this time frame while keeping the context of the longer-term market in mind. The market had broken a multiyear uptrend (7-Year Weekly Chart, figure 1.2) and was now retesting that upper range. The market had also built an inverted hammer right at the then sideways-to-downward-sloping fifty-week moving average. These were all longer-term, and therefore more reliable, signs of a shifting trend.

Section 2: Volume Confirmation

I also like to use ETFs at this stage to see whether trading volume confirms my thesis. The yen ETF arguably gave mixed signals and threw me off when I looked at this in real time, because the bounce off the 1st quarter of 2012 lows (117) was on low volume. This would be a confirmation of bearish action, but, as the yen stayed sticky in the upper range, volume started to pick up on the upside before and after the inverted hammer.

At this point I zoom into the daily charts to enter positions or to further monitor and time what's happening. From my publication, here is how I utilized the one-year chart on this same setup.

September 24 "The Tape" continued...

"Here's what the 1 year daily looks like, ascending bullish triangle, with an island reversal on high volume last week which created the inverted hammer on the weekly. Still trying to get a short on this but it definitely is tricky. The high on the inverted hammer is 127.36 on the ETF, or 77.15 on the Yen itself. I may take a shot if we get back there."

Figure 1.5

FXY, Japanese ETF, 2011–2012, Daily Chart

Section 3: Leveraged ETFs

Another market I like to watch when available is the leveraged ETF space. This can be on the same market or related ones. Note that this next strategy cannot be used in all markets and is contingent upon actually having additional ETFs in the space. I like to make sure there is decent liquidity and trading volume. There are no exact rules for this, but bid/ask spreads shouldn't be over five cents or so, and trading should be at least fifty thousand shares per day, in my opinion, to make the chart—or any trading data—relevant.

In the case of the yen, there is a double inverse yen ETF with the ticker symbol YCS. During the 3rd quarter of 2012, the YCS chart showed essentially what was expected, given the overall yen setup. That said, I like to look for additional volume or trading patterns, as markets don't always trade exactly inverse to each other. The following is a weekly chart for YCS from the same period in 2012.

Figure 1.6

YCS, Ultrashort Yen, 2009–2012, Weekly Chart

Figure 1.6 clearly shows declining downside momentum and declining downside volume, both of which are important indicators of a bottom. Since this instrument trades at two times the inverse of the currency, a base here means a top in the yen. Further, the same trading action as in the yen can be seen in the second

week of September, in this case a hammer at the basing low (inverse price action). Unfortunately, there were no volume "tells" other than a decline in downside selling pressure. This, too, could be viewed on the one-year daily chart for more detailed information.

Section 4: Seasonality

The last step I take is to look at a seasonality chart of the assets if one is available. In this case, I just wanted to know how the currency market trends during the season we were in. It is very important here to understand that the following yen chart is priced inverse to the yen charts I have used so far. So when the price rises, the yen is weakening, and when it falls, the yen is strengthening. This seasonal yen chart of the last thirty-five years shows average price trends during the year. As figure 1.7 shows, the yen tends to top in late July or early August (98.6 yen) and bottom in October (100.4 yen), both of which fit well with the setup.

Figure 1.7

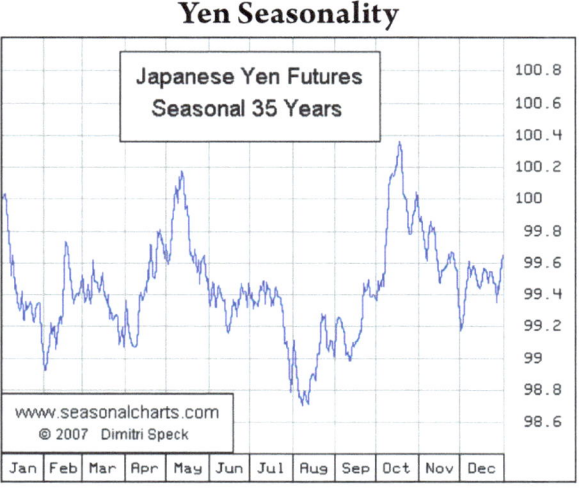

Section 5: Review

This level of detail, multiple market checks, and multiple time frames enables me to get a broad market view, and look for a major macro event, and then do top-down work to find investments based on risk tolerance and return requirements.

Review Process

Below is a quick review of the first steps to monitoring the main setup. From there, I move into the related market setups.

Yen Setup Process

1. Long-Term Monthly Chart (25+-Year, Wedge and Trend Line Indentify)
2. Long-Term Weekly Chart (7-Year Weekly, Trend Line and Moving Average)
3. Short Term Weekly Chart (2-Year Weekly, price action)
4. 1-Year Daily Chart (further analysis, position entry)
5. ETF Charts, (inverse, leveraged, volume and price action)
6. Seasonality Charts

Here is what the currency has done since then:

Figure 1.8

Japanese Yen 2008–2013

From September 2012 to December 2013, the market got absolutely hammered. The BOJ intervened in the market, increasing its asset purchases and removing caps on JGB purchasing. This was the fundamental driver, but the true setup was well in advance, prior to these interventions.

Chapter 2

RELATED ASSETS

Now I'll go back and look at additional technical methods using macroeconomic principles from the same time frame to enhance overall understanding of how markets work together. Though these charts and views were not in my published monthly work, they can dramatically improve overall confidence in larger macro set-ups. This step and process combines longer-term charting methods with economic relationships and principles.

Intermarket analysis is nothing new, but I like to use the same concepts and apply them to a longer-term chart basis and to monitor multiple sectors. Every macro relationship is different, so if a commodity rises, certain equity markets should, in theory, rise or some currencies should fall. If the level of a particular interest rate changes, it would be expected to impact certain exposed sectors, assets, or markets. When doing intermarket analysis, I like to first think about the major macro move of interest, list what some of the impacts would be if the move comes to pass, and then look at those spaces to see if there is confirming technical action taking place.

In this case, the yen weakening is itself nothing new, just a specific macro event that one can quantify and then look for evidence of its likelihood by monitoring where it would theoretically have impact. Let's walk through what an intervening Bank of Japan means to other assets in the space.

From a pure macro perspective, there are several fundamental impacts from this type of monetary policy. To keep things simple, I'll focus on the four most obvious. Currency cross rates, import markets, and foreign competitors can all be impacted as secondary components. For now, the following list focuses on the most obvious process, order, and initial impacts of BOJ intervention in their financial markets.

1. The Bank of Japan increases asset purchases
2. The Yen weakens
3. Domestic equity markets reflate
4. Bank balance sheets are bolstered
5. Domestic exporters' competitive advantage increases

Section 1: Index Charts

Equity Markets Reflate

The first place to look for price action confirming a potential weakening in the yen is the domestic equity market. A longer-term chart of the Nikkei Index shows almost the inverse of what was happening in the currency market. Although the index alone doesn't provide enough data, at the time, it did show a clear base forming.

Figure 2.1

Tokyo Nikkei Average, 2008–2012, Weekly Chart

The next thing to look at, as in the currency analysis, is the related ETF in the space (if available and liquid) so as to get a feel for volume patterns or any other additional price action that gives more insight. In this case EWJ and DXJ both represent the Tokyo Nikkei Average. The one important difference between these two is that DXJ hedges the underlying currency, whereas EWJ does not. For this analysis, I'll simply focus on DXJ, since hedging the currency risk is the preferred vehicle given the yen outlook.

Figure 2.2

DXJ, Wisdom Tree Hedged Equity ETF, 2008–2012, Weekly Chart

In this case the longer-term weekly chart showed price essentially in the same place as the underlying index. Within the weekly charts there wasn't much volume action that indicated anything other than that the base was continuing to build. This chart shows the basic construct even if the evidence was lacking. Let's move forward to show how to look for more detailed intermarket setups and technicals.

Section 2: Banks

The second item on the intermarket list, and arguably the sector most impacted by increased and aggressive BOJ policy, is the financial sector. The fact that a long-term uptrend in the yen puts pressure on financial stocks and strengthens the long-term bear in overall Japanese equities was well known. The yen, however, looked ready to fall, catalyzing events throughout the space. In my opinion, it is in this area that most market commentary fails to use market action in advance. These larger macro moves are already building in technical terms well before actual events, and if a trader knows what to look for, he or she can get ahead of them. By the time they are in the news, or have occurred, it is far too late.

At this stage, when a specific top-down process is identified but hasn't happened yet, I like to pull up a list of American Depository Receipts (ADRs) in specific sectors for the country I am analyzing for particular technical action. ADRs represent shares in foreign companies but are traded in the United States. They're usually on larger, better-known companies, as the listing requirements make issuing them favorable only for certain companies. As I switch my analysis to individual stocks, ADR generally s are the vehicle I use to apply techniques similar to those used for larger-scale analysis. This is exclusively for foreign market setups.

The main index ETF (DXJ, figure 2.2) provided little insight outside of a base formation; however, in this case we had three financial firms to take a closer look at, Mizuho Group(MFG), Mitsubishi Financial Group(MTU), and Nomura Holdings(NMR). The first step was to take a look at MTU on a monthly basis because it has the longest available price history and allowed had a more-than-twenty-year monthly chart. This is best thought of as being compared to the very first long-term yen chart, the multidecade monthly view.

Figure 2.3

Mitsubishi Financial Group, MTU 1990–2012, Monthly Chart

A few things in figure 2.3 stand out. First, from the 2008 low there is a clear base forming. Second, the hammer at the 2003 low is intact as the low for the decade. Third, there is a capitulation volume spike on the monthly without any real further decline in price. This capitulation volume is early in 2011. Finally, there is a clear downtrend that, though still intact, shows a definable place within the long-term chart indicating an important trend shift.

MTU Weekly 2004–2012

The next step is to zoom in on the nearer-term base as I did within the underlying currency market. It is important at this step to also change the time frames to a weekly chart. The multiyear weekly chart shows a few important points.

Figure 2.4

Mitsubishi Financial Group, MTU, 2004–2012, Weekly Chart

Important to note is that figure 2.4 shows that the 2009 low is intact (as seen in the monthly), the base pattern was clearly taking shape over the prior four years, and the fifty-week moving average was beginning to head up. Downside volume had dissipated, which is positive toward the end of a larger base structure.

The same weekly time frame for ADRs of the other two financials showed similar formations. Again, for these ADRs data was available only for nearer-term action. Those with access to more data, one can take all these steps for each issue vehicle being studied.

Figure 2.5

Mizuho Financial Group, MFG 2007–2012, Weekly Chart

As the MFG chart shows, there was not only a long-term five-year weekly wedge pattern that price had recently broken above, but the fifty-week moving average had clearly started to turn, and volume picked up nicely on the first breakout and pullback to the same fifty-week moving average.

Furthermore, the chart above shows that the momentum decline had slowed and was putting in a bullish divergence, the moving average was starting to turn up again, and a bullish crossover (fifty over two-hundred) looked likely.

Figure 2.6

Nomura Holdings, NMR 2007–2012, Weekly Chart

The last bank, Nomura Holdings (symbol NMR, figure 2.6), perhaps the most well known globally, illustrates the reason looking at more than one stock in the sector is helpful. Although the least developed in terms of bases, figure 2.6 shows that NMR was still in a declining wedge pattern, and the volume had dissipated so clearly that it really spoke to a lack of selling at these lower levels.

With the stocks so beaten up, the real risk felt more like a waiting game than a loss of principle. That said, waiting itself is an opportunity cost. Using the above analysis on the currency, traders can better time the catalyst, which is what this chapter is really about.

Section 3: Exporters

The fourth fundamental economic relationship affected by BOJ policy is between a weakening currency and increasing exporter competitiveness.

The technical process for examining exporters is essentially the same. The focus is still on ADRs, in this case for Toyota. Again, trends can be identified by looking first at the multidecade monthly chart. In Toyota's case it will show that the nearer-term (daily) views provided the most insight and essentially confirmed the relationship. Lets first start with the longer term monthly chart in figure 2.7.

Figure 2.7

Toyota Motors 20+ Year, Monthly Chart

The longer-term trend on the multidecade monthly chart (figure 2.7) was clearly up over the years. In 2008 and 2011 Toyota tested its long-term uptrend and held. The price had also moved above both the fifty- and two-hundred-month moving averages.

Weekly Charts

The next step is to shorten the time frames and look at the weekly charts. Here, I use a nearly ten-year weekly chart to get an idea of volume, candle patterns, and overall market information (figure 2.8).

Figure 2.8

Toyota Motors 2004–2012, Weekly Chart

The weekly chart (figure 2.8) showed Toyota approaching a bullish fifty-week moving average crossover of the two-hundred-week moving average, so the price was starting to move out of its base. This contrasted with the financials, which were still in their base structures. There was also a volume spike from earlier in 2012, as the price was supported by the fifty-week moving average.

The real insight came in the next step and final chart, the one-year daily chart (I did not review daily charts of the bank stocks, though that can clearly help). This chart (figure 2.9) focuses essentially on the price action above the monthly and weekly moving averages as seen in figures 2.7 and 2.8, but on a daily basis. Using shorter time frames after reviewing monthly and weeklies enables a good understanding of what is happening on the daily charts but within the broader context. Traditional, less stable daily indicators can be overlaid on the knowledge of what is happening within the longer time frames.

Figure 2.9

Toyota Motors 2011–2012, Daily Chart

The one-year daily chart above (figure 2.9) now reveals quite a bit. First, the trend support along the two-hundred-day moving average is clear. Many analysts get caught up with whether exact levels on daily charts are holding. When prices don't hold exactly at the right level, they tend to junk the entire chart or process. Trying to understand action in terms of stock stage (accumulation, uptrend, distribution, and downtrend) from a broader context when weekly and monthly levels are known provides focus on where the stock is likely to head in the bigger picture versus looking at just a few days of trading below a daily moving average.

Toyota slipped a bit below its two-hundred-day moving average in July at 72.04, but stayed well within the weekly and monthly moving averages (50 and 200). The same year of data in a weekly time frame chart (figure 2.10), reveals that the break of the two-hundred-day moving average (traditionally bearish) actually turns into a hammer at the fifty-week moving average (bullish).

Figure 2.10

Toyota Motors, 2002-2012, 1-Year Weekly Chart

The volume was also tremendous on the move in the 60 to 80 range, as can be seen clearly on both the daily and weekly charts. As the price built a second base in that range (60–80) during the first half of the year, the volume rose again on the test of the two-hundred-day moving average in late July. This type of price action coupled with what was known about the yen both technically and fundamentally speaks loudly in terms of probabilities. It's this combination of macro fundamentals, multi-time frame charting, and detailed technical analysis that helps create more reliable opportunities.

Chapter 3

RETURNS

The last section will look at how the markets played out. To keep things simple, I took price data over the year from the date of my original the publication, September 24th, 2012. I will keep the structure the same, first looking at the yen, the broad equity market, the financials, and lastly the exporters.

Section 1: Yen Performance a Year Later

The yen ended up collapsing in spectacular fashion. The move was historic in nature and drastically shifted asset prices throughout the financial markets. Here's a chart of the yen in the following year. As was seen in figure 1.7, the market moved quickly.

Figure 3.1

Japanese Yen, 2007–2013, Weekly Chart

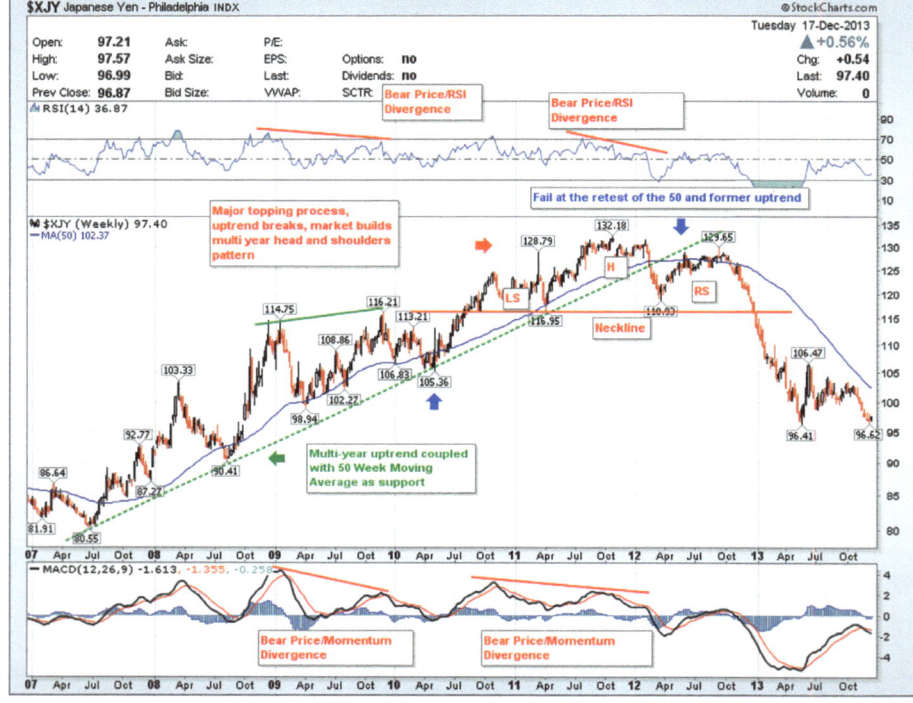

Section 2: Broad Market Returns

The broad equity markets benefited from this breakdown in the currency.

Figure 3.2

Tokyo Nikkei Average Daily Chart, September 2012–September 2013

Figure 3.2 shows the broad indexes from the lows in September to the highs in May 2013. The market moved from a low of 8488 to a high of 15942, or in other words, the broad equity index in Japan rallied in incredible 60+ percent in just under eight months. Figure 3.3 shows the weekly chart and puts the move into longer-term context.

Figure 3.3

Nikkei Average Weekly Chart, 2008–2013

Section 3: Bank Stock Returns

The next step is to look at how the financial stocks perform relative to the market and the currency. When using these intermarket setups, it's often unclear whether to trade the currency short, the leveraged instrument on the currency, individual ADRs, or try to pick what might be the best-performing sector or stock. My work so far shows that it seems to be different every time. However, one thought I've had on this in the past is to choose simply by the best-known name in the country. That said, I have seen in some of my work on sectors or sentiment trades where simply buying the ETF that covers the broadest indexes results in the best performance. This is an area I continue to study in depth as macro set ups come in many different types, and there are every increasing products designed to gain different types of exposure.

For simplicity's sake, I've put the three bank stocks on one chart for the year holding period to look at the post-yen collapse return data.

NMR led all banks in price performance. Figure 3.5 shows a price comparison for the following twelve months (9/24/12-9/24/13) on NMR, MTU, and MFG (figure 3.4). The green line is NMR, which significantly outperformed.

Figure 3.4

NMR, MTU, MFG, DXJ 1 Year Daily Performance Chart

Section 4: Exporter Returns

The last step is to look at the exporters' performance. In this case that was Toyota, which also broke out to over 130, as shown in figure 3.5.

Figure 3.5

Toyota Motors, Daily Chart, 2012–2013

Here is what that move looked like on the weekly chart. Figure 3.6 shows the long-term view on Toyota during the year the yen moved to the downside.

Figure 3.6

Toyota Motors, Weekly Chart 2008–2013

The last chart shows the Nikkei, DXJ, NMR, and TM to determine top performance by major assets in the space. In the end, NMR led all assets by moving uprising over 150 percent. The ETF DXJ tracked the index the expected way, as the underlying currency was hedged. Finally, TM also tracked the index very closely, moving up approximately 70 percent in the twelve months following the yen top.

Figure 3.7

1-Year Price Performance 2012–2013

Summary

By utilizing long-term charts, including macroeconomic relationships and inter-market analysis, we can better time important setups. Further, incorporating ETFs, leveraged ETFs, ADRs, and equity indexes we can add more price action and volume to the overall data sets, in order to confirm investment ideas.

This publication serves many roles. It outlines my process, shows my past successes, and highlights the advanced nature of my firm's work. My site, topdown-technicals.com, provides a macro chart monitor that has multi time frame views of all major assets, updated on a regular basis. My investment publication "The Tape," as highlighted above, is also available for purchase and is published on a monthly basis. "The Tape" serves to highlight opportunities like those discussed above and reviews all four major asset classes in a diligent and professional manner.

Finally, this publication on the yen also serves as the starting point for a larger market observation series that will include more market setups, including trading extreme sentiment, sector breakouts, market volatility, and leveraged ETFs. These will available in the near future as I continue to use these setups for my own macro work, as well as document them for readers and for those looking to increase their overall market awareness.